Whispers of Nature
Advanced Coloring Book

forces and other
ethereal beings

(for adults)

-Vol. 2-

~

Always, for my mom, Mirta, and dad, José Luis.
You are my source of inspiration and knowledge.
Thank you for believing in me.
I love you.

~

Hi there!

First of all … Thank you for choosing this book!

In the next pages you will find 30 original artworks waiting for you to bring them to life with colors or shades.

Tools of the trade: graphite pencils, colored pencils, markers, highlighters, pens and pastels. Feel free to trace the artwork into a thicker water resistant paper for watercolor paint.

Quick note for beginners:

- The magic happens when you blend and mix colors together. Don't just settle for the basic colors on your box set! You can mix up to three or four colored pencils if you only press lightly on the paper to avoid early saturation. Play with pressure to get different intensities.

- If you are working with shades of grey, remember the power of contrasts! At the end, check if the darkest spot is indeed the darkest, if not, don't be afraid to make shadows dark, it will bring quite a pop to your piece.

Also, you will find that all the pages are one sided should you want to cut your amazing colored/shaded art and frame it. Note that the number and title of each piece is at the back of each page.

Why do this?

You color or shade to give your mind a pleasing break away from all the work, the spreadsheets, the dishes, graphs, laundry, taxes and all those little joys of life that require you to have multiple trains of thought in only one railway. And when you hit that "I'm going to take a moment for myself and color because I want to/ I need to", you will find yourself concentrating just into one task.

And even though it's not the simplest of tasks –you actually have to make some chromatic decisions in the process- it is enough to let your mind take it down a notch and focus on the shapes, the lines, the spaces, the contrasts, the lights, the shadows… and soon you'll begin to give in to the moment, to actually be 100% coloring/shading and think of nothing else. You will be with yourself.

It's usually on times like these that your mind can stop worrying and relax, do some internal work, reorganize itself, clear the mental fog. All thanks to having to focus on a simple task that demands just the right amount of attention.

And suddenly, while debating which grey to use or whether green is an option or if you should just stick to blue for a while, a snippet of thought might come to mind, something that may sound silly at first, but the more you think of it the more meaning you get out of it and helps put things in perspective, and a new problem-solving idea is formed. This isn't magic. It's all you.

In a nutshell:

> *"Life is not complex. We are complex. Life is simple, and the simple thing is the right thing."*
> —Oscar Wilde

When you are stuck in a complex problem you better steer to doing simple things –like coloring/shading a book among other pleasurable tasks-. This is because THE SIMPLE reflects all the forces of nature that are also present on THE COMPLEX. Your intuition will let you see how things work in the simple scale and build a mental bridge to transfer these forces to the complex scale.

… So what are you waiting for?

This is a blank page for you to try your coloring/shading tools on.

- Sometimes they react differently depending on the paper. Try blending colors and experiment with mixing different tools. Go wild!

- If you use markers or other wet media, remember to place a paper behind the drawing to avoid bleed through accidents on the next drawing.

This is a blank page for you to try your coloring/shading tools on.

This is a blank page for you to try your coloring/shading tools on.

← **1. Realities**

(... or your own title based on your interpretation: ....)

← 2. Hunt

(or your own interpretation: ....)

← 3. Transition

(or your own interpretation: ....)

← **4. Hunger**
(or your own interpretation: ....)

← **5. Touch**
  (or your own interpretation: ....)

← **6. Break Through**
(or your own interpretation: ....)

7. Whirl
(or your own interpretation: ....)

← 8. Universe
(or your own interpretation: ....)

← **9. Embrace**
(or your own interpretation: ....)

10. Collision
(or your own interpretation: ....)

← **11. Anima**
    (or your own interpretation: ....)

12. Beacon
(or your own interpretation: ....)

← 13. Tension

(or your own interpretation: ....)

14. Senses
(or your own interpretation: ....)

← **15. Momentum**
(or your own interpretation: ....)

16. Thread
(or your own interpretation: ....)

← 17. Potential
(or your own interpretation: ....)

← **18. Impulse**
   (or your own interpretation: ....)

← 19. Counterpart

(or your own interpretation: ....)

← 20. Compression
(or yourown interpretation: ....)

21. Ritual
(or your own interpretation: ....)

22. Dance
(or your own interpretation: ....)

 **23. Sound**
(or your own interpretation: ....)

 **24. Bravery**
(or your own interpretation: ....)

25. Void
(or your own interpretation: ....)

26.Sleep
(or your own interpretation: ....)

26.Sleep
(or your own interpretation: ....)

← **27. Depth**
  (or your own interpretation: ....)

28. Barrier
(or your own interpretation: ....)

29. Grasp
(or your own interpretation: ....)

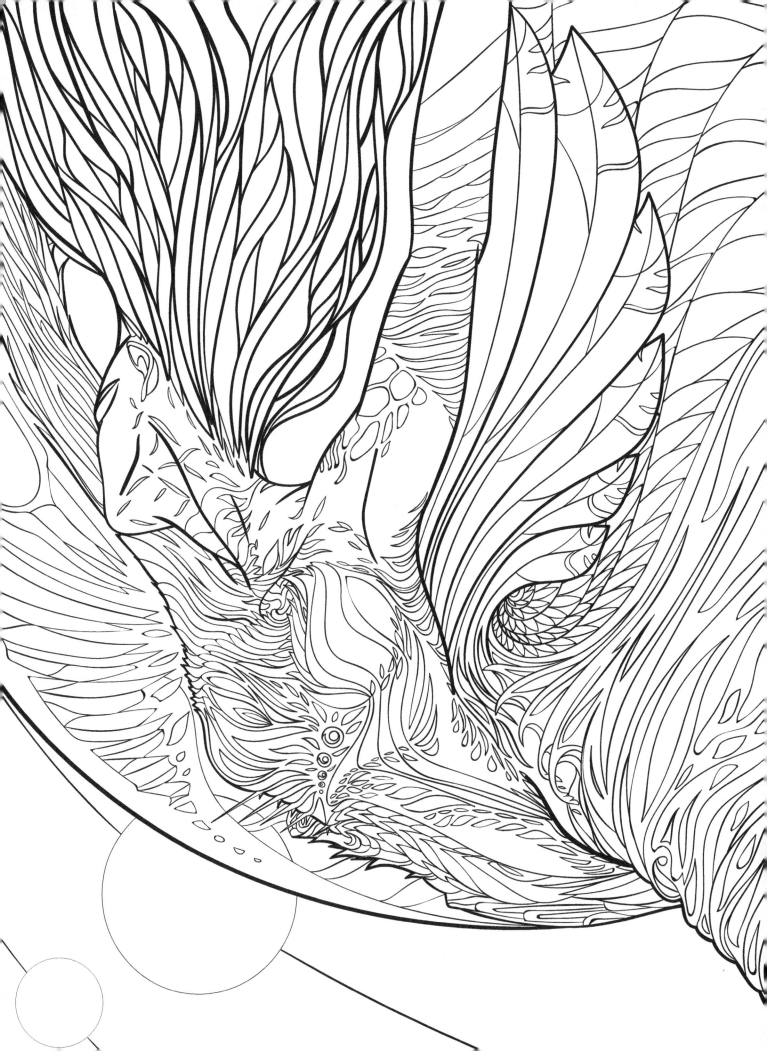

← 30. Force of Life
(or your own interpretation: ....)

Hello there!

I invite you to write in this space any memories that come to mind and any feelings or emotions that coloring a certain artwork may evoke. Don't forget to write the number or name of the piece! -it's on the back of each page-

Well, ... I hope you've liked this journey!

And I'd love to hear from you! Did you enjoy the book? Also, I invite you to share with me your colored/shaded pieces -I can't wait to see them! So, tag me in any photo you take or send an email (contact info at the end of the page). By the way, don't forget to write your customer review on Amazon!

This book is also available in Spanish, under the title:
"Susurros de la Naturaleza Libro Avanzado para Colorear: Fuerzas y otros seres etéreos."

You can also check out the first and third volumes of this series:

Vol.I

"Masked nymphs and other ethereal beings"

Vol.III

"Darklings and other ethereal beings"

A little bit about me:

Hi!- I'm Antonella, a self-published illustrator & advertising graduate, based in Argentina. You can find me on social media as "@userantonella". Follow me on instagram where my imaginary cat and I post some artistic behind the scenes images & videos!

Born in Argentina, I moved with my family when I was 10 to live in Peru, Spain, Brazil and returned to Argentina at 24. And although throughout these years I'd been devoted to various fields of study –hospitality, architecture, languages, creative writing and advertising- art has been the strongest constant throughout my life.

About the Whispers of Nature series, I married the best of both worlds: traditional handmade designs and digital vector art. Each of my artworks begun as a lovely (yet messy) hand-drawn pencil sketch before using the computer to amplify these images to a comfortable size for accurate vector tracing, yet keeping the pleasing traditional art flavor thanks to the digital pen.

As for the decision to make this kind of book (coloring books), I confess that it responds to a deep need to focus the mind and meditate using art, since in today's world it is easy to become anxious about anything and everything. I let my creativity wander free and began to feel certain currents and flows, forces that push and rise, pull and connect, spiral inwards and outwards. It was those forces that I translated (as best as I could) in my drawings here, and my interpretation of them is what I wanted to share with you.

I hope you found this book as pleasurable as can be!

 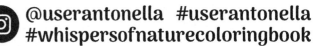

userantonella@gmail.com

@userantonella #userantonella
#whispersofnaturecoloringbook

Made in United States
North Haven, CT
27 January 2022